ACCOUNTING

THE 2ND OLDEST PROFESSION

ATOP AURORA'S DECAGON

S. Aurora Riel Grimes

Table of Contents

Accounting:

The 2nd Oldest Profession

ACCT 101

By: S. Aurora Riel Grimes

PREFACE

I have called this volume, ACCT 101, 1st in this series on **Accounting**. In MGT 101, I discussed **Management**, which I claim to be the Oldest Profession. Here, I discuss **Accounting**, which I claim to be the 2nd Oldest Profession, a profession that aims to serve **Management**.

For a given series, I recommend that the reader follow the sequencing to understand and enjoy better the topics that are covered.

It is my hope that you read other volumes in this and other series, as I share my thoughts on many topics from **Management** to **Accounting** to Historic Maragondon, where Villa Cecilia is. And yes, I also have volumes on or relating to Aurora's Decagon.

Accounting:
The 2nd Oldest Profession

In MGT 101, I first invited you to look at the Introduction and the first two chapters of **GENESIS**, the first Book of the Holy Bible. And then I shared with you passages I had selected from various parts of the Bible that relate to **Management**, **Economics**, and decision-making.

Thru MGT 101. I also claim that you and I are among **The LORD** 's appointed stewards or **Managers**. As **Managers**, it behooves us to learn **Accounting** and about **Accounting**, if it aims to serve us, as **Management**.

ACCOUNTING AIMS TO SERVE MANAGEMENT

Accounting aims to serve **Management**, in relation to its tasks, namely, **PODC,** and in relation to its responsibilities as a steward. You may ask, which Manager can claim s/he could do **Management** well without **Accounting?**

Let's visit **GENESIS** again. In the 2nd chapter, we heard it loud and clear: (where I claim **Management** became the 1st and oldest profession).

The LORD God then took the man and settled him in the garden of Eden, **to cultivate and care for it.**

The LORD God gave the man this order: You are **free to eat** from any of the trees of the garden **except the tree** of knowledge of good and evil... I will make a helper suited to him… **The LORD God** brought them to the man to see what he would call them; whatever the man called each living creature was then its name… **The LORD God** then built the rib that he had taken from the man into a woman.

THE GARDEN OF EDEN

The LORD had already called the man to **manage Creation**.

Now the snake was the most cunning of all the wild animals that **The LORD God** had made. He asked the woman, "Did God really say, 'You shall **not eat from any of the trees** in the garden'?"

The snake used a lie to engage the woman, to gather information, and possibly to gain control, for this is really not what **The LORD** said…The woman answered the snake: "We may eat of the fruit of the trees in the garden; it is **only about the fruit of the tree in the middle of the garden** that God said, 'You shall not eat it or even touch it, or else you will die.'"

But the snake said to the woman: "You certainly will not die! God knows well that when you eat of it your eyes will be opened and you will be like gods, who know good and evil."

The snake took control by acting like he had more and better information which the woman accepted…The woman who listened to the snake was sold that the tree was good for food and pleasing to the eyes, and the tree was desirable for gaining wisdom. She took some of its fruit and ate it; and she also gave some to her husband, who was with her, and he ate it.

ACCOUNTING: EXPLANATION

The LORD knew where they were. But He called and was asking the Man. **The LORD** wanted **Accounting** or **explanation** from the man and his wife.

Adam answered, "I heard you in the garden; but I was afraid, because I was naked, so I hid." (The professional **Accounting** term for hiding is *concealment*.) What is **Accounting**, but **explanation**. **The LORD** knew what they did. **The LORD** knew where they were hiding. He knew what they had done before they decided to hide. But He asked Adam and Eve questions nonetheless as

He demanded **explanation** that we now professionally call *Accounting.*

We may ask: Who is entitled to **Accounting** or **explanation**? We have recognized that anyone who entrusted another with resources of any type could and should demand **explanation** relating to such entrusted resources. (Our **Accounting** term or code for these resources that satisfy our definition requirements is *ASSETS*.)

ACCOUNTING. ENTAILS IMP

Explanation entails **IMP:** **I**dentifying, **M**easuring, and **P**resenting details about such resources.

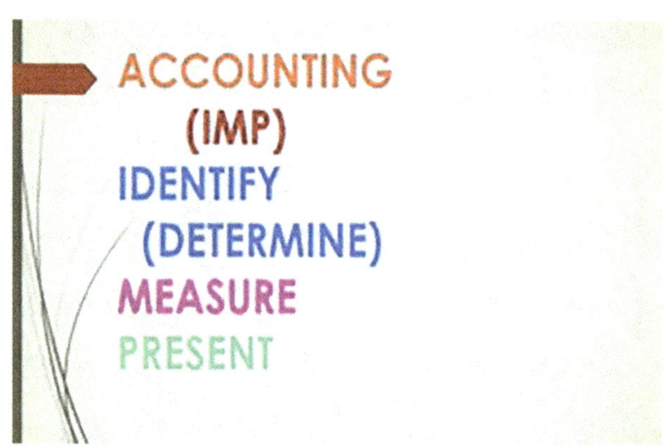

THE PARABLE OF
THE TALENTS

The LORD says, "It will be as when a man who is going on a journey called in his servants and entrusted his possessions to them. To one, he gave five talents; to another, two; to a third, one-- to each according to his ability.

Then he went away... After a long time, the master of those servants came back and settled accounts with them. The one who had received five talents came forward bringing the additional five… He said, 'Master, you gave me five talents. See, I have made five more.' …His master said to him, 'Well done, my good and faithful servant. Since you were faithful in small matters, I will give you great responsibilities. Come, share your master's joy.'

[Then] the one who had received two talents also came forward and said, 'Master, you gave

me two talents. See, I have made two more.' …
His master said to him, 'Well done, my good and
faithful servant. Since you were faithful in small
matters, I will give you great responsibilities.
Come, share your master's joy.'

Then the one who had received the one
talent came forward and said, 'Master, I knew
you were a demanding person, harvesting where
you did not plant and gathering where you did
not scatter; so, out of fear I went off and buried
your talent in the ground. Here it is back.' …His
master said to him in reply, 'You wicked, lazy
servant! So, you knew that I harvest where I did
not plant and gather where I did not scatter?

Should you not then have put my money
in the bank so that I could have got it back with
interest on my return? …Now then! Take the
talent from him and give it to the one with ten.
For to everyone who has, more will be given
and he will grow rich; but from the one who
has not, even what he has will be taken away…
And throw this useless servant into the darkness
outside, where there will be wailing and grinding
of teeth.'

The LORD does not intend for humans to act with impunity. Man was given limited dominion over creation. Limits were set and they are expected to be observed and adhered to.

There will be days of reckoning and days of judgment. It will be at **The LORD**'s own time, not ours, but He definitely has "**Responsibility Accounting**" in mind. Equality and justice are foremost in God's concept of **Accounting** and **Accountability.**

ACCOUNTING SERVES MANAGEMENT

Accounting aims to enable and serve **Management**. **Accounting** aims to:

1) provide information for various uses and purposes of decision-makers

2) provide information to those entitled and have rights to receive such information, to uncover or do disclosures

   a) of those events that are illegitimately attempted to be concealed and covered up, and

   b) of those who attempt to "pass the buck," if only to escape responsibility.

3) use systematically codes (**Accounts,** and **Chart of Accounts**, where they

keep out of sight of the unauthorized the definitions of the codes or **Accounts**) to limit dissemination or to withhold confidential information from those who do not have rights to such information.

We were able to see what anomalies and irregularities had transpired from the moment that cunning serpent entered the scene in the Garden. The serpent started asking questions and the woman started answering and providing it information. Was the serpent entitled to such information?

Accounting as a profession tries 1) to prevent anomalies, 2) to uncover anomalies, if any, and 3) to report on effects of anomalies that may have occurred.

ACCOUNTING BY TYPES OF USERS

Accounting can be classified by types of users:

1) **FINANCIAL,**
2) **MANAGERIAL,** **and**
3) **COMPLIANCE.**

ACCOUNTING BY TIME FRAME

Accounting data may be classified by time frame:

a) **HISTORIC** or past (like yearly reports which may or may not be certified)

b) **CURRENT** or real time (like on- going reporting for different projects, jobs or product costing), and—as these are internal, they are not certified.

c) **FUTURE** or forecasts, budgeted, or projected are internal, not certified.

ACCOUNTING IS MICRO-ECONOMICS

Accounting is **basically** interested in **Micro-Economics** (business units or firms). These business units are individually called, **Entity**, the **unit of focus** in **Accounting**.

The **center of gravity** for **Accounting** as for **Management**, is **Economics**.

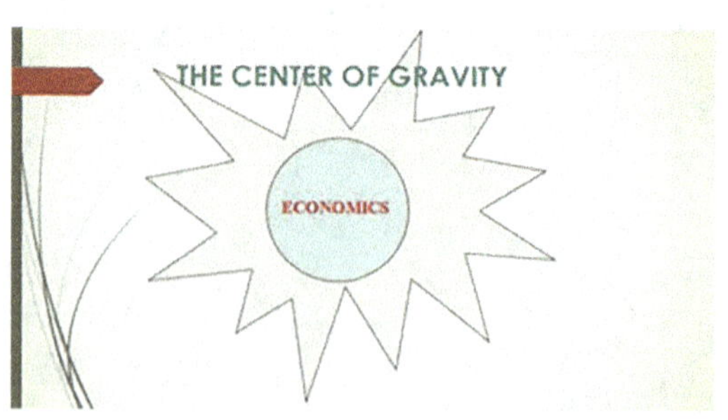

Thus, most **explanations** provided by **Accounting** are about **Economic** activities and effects. **Accounting** aims to do **(IMP) I**dentify **or determine, M**easure, **and P**resent **Economic** resources.

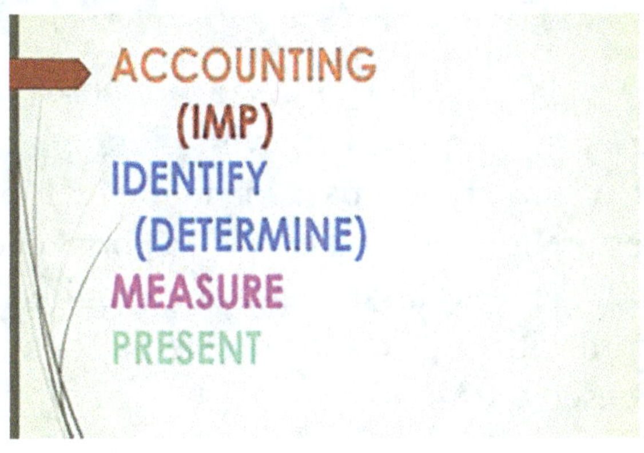

Accounting for businesses involves **Micro-Economics**. **Economics** relating to complex societal, industry, or governmental units or **Macro-Economics** normally requires **SPECIAL TYPE** of **Accounting** that is relegated to other Standards setters.

FINANCIAL ACCOUNTING

FINANCIAL Accounting focuses on a **micro-economic** Entity, with Economics, as center of gravity, on past, or **historical** events. As they are for external users, Reports rendered by Management as stewards are required to be in accord with GAAP and are certified or attested by licensed **CPAs.**

Reports are intended to be used by outsiders who stakeholders and owners or stockholders, whether past, present, or potential. The certification or attestation of independent Accountants in regard to GAAP is intended to lend credibility to the reports so that outsiders could trust that such reports are not subject to manipulations of Management (the reporting stewards).

GAAP

GAAP are **Accounting practices** that are with *substantial authoritative support*. This means that a recognized body of **Professional Accountants** adopted such practices, which are then promulgated through their published official pronouncements.

DISCLOSURE PRINCIPLE: 1st GAAP

Accounting provides **explanation**, on **Economic** resources and activities that need to be 1) **I**dentified or determined, 2) **M**easured, and 3) **P**resented (**IMP**) in accord with the 1st pervasive **GAAP**, i.e., **DISCLOSURE PRINCIPLE.**

In the Garden, after succumbing to the serpent's invitation (or temptation), the eyes of both of them were opened, and they knew that they were naked; <u>so, they sewed fig leaves together and</u> <u>made loincloths for themselves.</u>

They did a <u>**cover-up.**</u> Precisely, this is the 1st instinct of those who commit irregular acts. They try to do additional acts that might make it difficult for others to follow their irregular or criminal tracks; difficult for others to know what they had done. Understandably, <u>**cover up**</u>

is what makes **Accounting** even more necessary (imperative) and important.

Accounting means **explanation** or **DISCLOSURE** (uncovering), the opposite of, or an **antidote** for <u>a cover up</u>. **IMP** has become an integral part of the **DISCLOSURE PRINCIPLE.**

When they heard the sound of **The LORD God** walking about in the garden at the breezy time of the day, the man and his wife hid themselves from **The LORD God** behind the trees of the garden.

People may hide their bad acts. They may physically hide or remove themselves from the crime scene to possibly avoid responsibility, making the CSI, a bit difficult and complicated. Adam and Eve hid themselves behind the trees in the garden, with leaves to effect a **cover-up**, in **Accounting** parlance, **concealment.**

It is not unusual for people to steal and then disappear from the locality, in **Accounting** language, to have **absconded**. This word is related to the word *escondido*, Spanish for hidden. So, thieves may hide their acts, by concealment or they may escape and leave the neighborhood or community, in effect, **absconding**.

Accounting aims to disclose (**uncover**) what may be hidden (or **concealed**). It also aims to explain a cover-up, and method applied, whether physical or through records manipulation, forgeries, and fraud.

DISCLOSURE PRINCIPLE, the 1st PERVASIVE GAAP requires explanation of the nature and the effect on the Financial Reports of *any violation of law, policy, and any other GAAP.*

VERIFIABILITY PRINCIPLE- 2ND GAAP

Reports could be mere allegations or claims. There is need to establish the **truth** (through **proof** or **confirmation**) to make the Reports believable or trustworthy.

Accounting prefers independent and separate sources of information and different ways of knowing about the events, using documents, computations, statements of disinterested parties, testimonies that would cure any suspicion of conflicts of interest and hidden agendas that could blemish the truth.

Veritas, **ver**acity, and **ver**ify (with root **ver**) relate to establishing the truth that parties can agree on as facts, even in their absence and as many tend to easily forget, and may have conflicting views, interests, and perceptions.

These are all parts of the 2ⁿᵈ pervasive **GAAP** of **VERIFIABILITY.**

In the Garden, Adam provided an **explanation.** Similarly, Eve provided an **explanation**. There was no indication of contradiction in their claims, although they spoke and had two different partial versions of what happened.

Let's look closer at the issue of **VERIFIABILITY** and lack of it.

In the Garden, God asked: Who told you that you were naked? Have you eaten from the tree of which I had forbidden you to eat?

The LORD continued to ask despite His knowledge of everything. This is to demand an **explanation** (an **Accounting**). The man replied, "The woman whom you put here with me-- she gave me fruit from the tree, so I ate it."

The man was "*passing the buck*" (*finger pointing* to the woman) possibly to escape responsibility for his action or violation. People tend to **pass the buck** to **deflect attention**, to remove the focus on themselves and to direct attention to others.

The man directs attention to the woman. **The LORD God** then asked the woman: What is this you have done?

The LORD continued to ask despite His knowledge of everything to demand an explanation from another source of data and information (for **verification** and for confirmation or refutation of Adam's claims or allegations)- **The LORD** demands an Accounting.

So, **The LORD** had another source of information to establish the **truth** or **veracity** of the initial information. VERIFIABILITY is a need for **proof** and **confirmation**, for **evidence** to **support** or to **refute** what may have been observed or asserted.

Accounting students soon realize that most of their activities will hinge on **verification** and **confirmation.** It is not enough to hear what someone says or claims. There has to be some

other statements and **documents** that could separately help **establish the truth or untruth** of a statement or claim. To **verify** means to establish the **truth;** to **confirm** is to agree (preferably from a different or **independent source**) as to the truth of a statement or claim.

Accounting students learn the differences between data, assumptions, presumptions, inferences. implications, conclusions, information, facts, opinions and should readily reject the existence of such **ultra-moronic** oxymoron **ALTERNATIVE FACTS.**

They learn about different sources and different ways of gathering information, better than allowing and readily accepting what are **unsubstantiated (unsupported)** claims or allegations.

Students learn about the pervasive **GAAP** of **VERIFIABILITY,** as they study more about this profession where the goal is explanation. *Verifiability is the ability to be established as true* from different sources and in different ways.

Accountants are interested in the **veracity** or truth of items or events, to the extent that the **items or events can be shown to exist**, and to the extent **that they can be measured** through generally accepted **Procedures**.

The woman answered, "The snake tricked me, so I ate it."

The woman was also ***passing the buck*** maybe to avoid responsibility by **deflecting attention** to someone else. But, no one is disputing her claim, so her **undisputed** claims may be deemed or **presumed to be true.** As her claims did not **dispute** Adam's claims, such may be also deemed or **presumed to be true.**

But with **The LORD**, no one does wrong with **impunity** (capacity or ability to escape punishment). **Accounting** comes with responsibility and **ACCOUNTABILITY,** and with consequences of doing bad decisions, actions or violations.

With two separate testimonies (from Adam and Eve) out of three possible statements or sources (from Adam, Eve and the snake), in the **absence of contradiction**, the statements may be **taken as verified and confirmed**.

All three were **indicted** and out came the **verdict**, followed by the Lord's **sentencing** and corresponding **punishments**.

Then the **Lord God** said to the snake: "Because you have done this, cursed are you among all the animals, tame or wild; On your belly you shall crawl, and dust you shall eat all the days of your life."

So, the Lord sentenced and punished all three of them individually and separately.

ANOTHER INSTANCE OF VERIFICATION

In Daniel 13, Susanna, very delicate and beautiful, was veiled; but those transgressors of the law ordered that she be exposed so as to sate themselves with her beauty. All her companions and the onlookers were weeping.

In the midst of the people the two old men rose up and laid their hands on her head. As she wept, she looked up to heaven, for she trusted in the Lord wholeheartedly…The old men said, "As we were walking in the garden alone, this woman entered with two servant girls, shut the garden gates and sent the servant girls away…A young man, who was hidden there, came and lay with her. When we, in a corner of the garden, saw this lawlessness, we ran toward them. We saw them lying together, but the man we could not hold, because he was stronger than us; he opened the gates and ran off…Then we seized this one and asked who the young man was, but she refused to tell us. We **testify** to this." …The assembly believed them, since they were elders and judges of the people, and they **condemned** her to death.

[In this case, two old men submitted only one crime. They had a unified claim, with them together as the witnesses to a crime.]

But Susanna cried aloud: "Eternal God, you know what is hidden and are aware of all things before they come to be: you know that they have testified falsely against me. Here I am about to die, though I have done none of the things for which these men have condemned me."

The Lord heard her prayer. As she was being **led to execution**, God stirred up the holy spirit of a young boy named Daniel, and he cried aloud: "I am **innocent** of this woman's blood." All the people turned and asked him, "What are you saying?" …He stood in their midst and said, "Are you such fools, you Israelites, to **condemn** a daughter of Israel without **investigation** and without clear **evidence**? Return to court, for they have **testified falsely** against her." …Then all the people returned in haste. To Daniel the elders said, "Come, sit with us and inform us, since God has given you the prestige of old age."

But he replied, "**Separate** these two far from one another, and I will **examine** them." After they were separated from each other, he called one of them and said: "How you have grown evil with age! Now have your past sins come to term: passing unjust sentences, condemning the innocent, and **freeing the guilty**, although the Lord says, 'The innocent and the just you shall not put to death.'…Now, then, if you were a **witness**, tell me under what tree you saw them together." "Under a mastic tree," he answered… "Your fine **lie has cost you your head**," said Daniel; "for the angel of God has already received the sentence from God and shall split you in two." …Putting him to one side, he ordered the other one to be brought. "Offspring of Canaan, not of Judah," Daniel said to him, "beauty has seduced you, lust has perverted your heart. This is how you acted with the daughters of Israel, and in their fear they yielded to you; but a daughter of Judah did not tolerate your lawlessness. Now, then, tell me under what tree you surprised them together." …"Under an oak," he said. "Your fine lie has cost you also your head," said Daniel; "for the angel of God waits with a sword to cut you in two so as to destroy you both." …The whole assembly cried aloud, blessing God who saves those who hope in him. They rose up against the two old men, for by their own words Daniel had **convicted them of bearing false witness** …They condemned them to the fate they had planned for their neighbor: in accordance with the law of Moses they put them to death. Thus, was innocent blood spared that day.

[There was one accused, innocent Susanna that prevailed over two lying old male **conspirators** as witnesses with cancelling testimonies. Truth wins over plurality or frequency of claims.]

MATERIALITY PRINCIPLE- 3RD GAAP

Accountants always say that in Accounting, we deal only with things that are important or Material. What is important or Material? What is unimportant or Immaterial, and therefore, Irrelevant or de minimis?

THE POOR WIDOW'S CONTRIBUTION

He (The Lord) sat down opposite the treasury and observed how the crowd put money into the treasury. Many rich people put in large sums, **Absolutely Material**…A poor widow also came and put in two small coins worth a few cents…Calling His disciples to Himself, He said to them, "Amen, I say to you, this poor widow put in **more than all the other** contributors to the treasury…For they have all contributed from their **surplus wealth**, but she, from her poverty, has contributed all she had, **her whole livelihood**," **Relatively Material.**

The Lord taught us about **Relative Materiality.** In **Accounting,** we have occasions to decide when one is relevant and not the other. **Absolute** (large amounts) vs **Relative Materiality** (large %).

CONSISTENCY PRINCIPLE- 4TH GAAP

Let's get back to GENESIS. We left off where the Lord demanded **Accounting**, from the man and the woman. They were made accountable for their violations. **The Lord** punished the snake, the woman, and the man. To the snake He said: "I will put enmity between you and the woman, and between your offspring and hers; They will strike at your head, while you strike at their heel."

To the woman He said: "I will intensify your toil in childbearing; in pain you shall bring forth children. Yet your urge shall be for your husband, and he shall rule over you."

To the man He said: "Because you listened to your wife and ate from the tree about which I commanded you; You shall not eat from it.

Cursed is the ground because of you! In toil you shall eat its yield all the days of your life. Thorns and thistles it shall bear for you, and you shall eat the grass of the field. By the sweat of your brow you shall eat bread, until you return to the ground, from which you were taken; for you are dust, and to dust you shall return."

The man gave his wife the name "Eve," because she was the mother of all the living.

Besides the punishment, the **Lord God** made for the man and his wife garments of skin, with which he clothed them. [This is where Abraham Maslow's Need Hierarchy started shaping up, with the 1st 2 elements. The Lord first provided man and woman FOOD, and now, CLOTHING. This will be covered in another volume.]

The Lord God therefore banished him from the garden of Eden, to till the ground from which he had been taken…He expelled the man, stationing the cherubim and the fiery revolving sword east of the garden of Eden, to guard the way to the tree of life…Adam and Eve were expelled from Eden. Adam was earlier given dominion over most of the creation. But along with Eve, he was punished, and expelled from Eden, but not without any **Accounting**.

OUTSIDE THE GARDEN OF EDEN

Man and woman later had two sons, each with their activities and own organization…Cain was a farmer, tiller of the ground. Abel was a shepherd, tender of a flock…In the course of time Cain brought an offering to **The LORD** from the fruit of the ground, while Abel, for his part, brought the fatty portion of the firstlings of his flock… **The LORD** looked with favor on Abel and his offering, but on Cain and his offering He did not look with favor. So, Cain was very angry and dejected.

Then **The LORD** said to Cain: Why are you angry? Why are you dejected? If you act rightly, you will be accepted; but if not, sin lies in wait at the door: its urge is for you, yet you can rule over it.

Again, **The LORD** knew what was happening, yet He asked Cain for **explanation** – (**Accounting**). But Cain did not explain…Cain said to his brother Abel, "Let us go out in the field." When they were in the field, Cain attacked his brother Abel and killed him. Again, **The LORD** knew what was happening, yet He asked Cain for **explanation**, (**Accounting**). But Cain did not explain.

Then **The LORD** asked Cain, "Where is your brother Abel?" …But Cain did not explain, either. He refused to do any **Accounting.** He answered, "I do not know. Am I my brother's keeper?"

But **nothing** can be hidden from **The LORD**. Cain's failure to do **Accounting** did not free him of his **Accountability.** With **The LORD**, we cannot do things with impunity. No amount of concealment and denial would work with Him.

God then said: What have you done? Your brother's blood cries out to me from the ground! …Now you are banned from the ground that opened its mouth to receive your brother's blood from your hand… If you till the ground, it shall no longer give you, its produce. You shall become a constant wanderer on the earth…Cain said to **The LORD**: "My punishment is too great to bear. Look, you have now banished me from the ground. I must avoid you and be a constant wanderer on the earth. Anyone may kill me at sight."

Cain complained about the punishment, while the man and the woman in the Garden of Eden did not complain. Maybe it was truly a greater punishment, telling us life is much greater than a forbidden fruit.

Now, in both cases, the culprits were made Accountable, and were punished. This is where we learned the importance of the **GAAP** of **CONSISTENCY.**

Consistency in **Accounting** means that if we accept a procedure as fitting and wise to use, we **follow through with the same procedure from period to period**. We **do not whimsically** change from one procedure to another. We **do not arbitrarily** use a procedure and then change to another with no rhyme or reason. We adopt a procedure and if we feel justified to use it, we turn it to be our intended one and stick to it or **adhere to it from one period to the next**, like policy.

We saw earlier that Adam and Eve and the snake got their deserved punishments for their evil deeds. So did Cain. In simple terms, if a method or practice has been adopted, the **CONSISTENCY PRINCIPLE** requires that it be applied to similar circumstances that follow from period to period. **Consistency** frowns upon whimsical and arbitrary changes in applications, preferences, and **Procedures**. **Consistency** requires us to follow through with our set policies and defined **Procedures** from period to period (year to year). To render this **GAAP** effective, all important and **material deviations (inconsistencies)** would require a special **explanation** or proper **disclosure** (the 1st Pervasive **GAAP**) of the **change** and the **effect of the change**.

ECONOMICS, MANAGEMENT, & ACCOUNTING

So, when **The LORD** gave Adam dominion over creation, **The LORD** called Adam to do **Management**, the 1st and oldest profession... As **The LORD** demanded **explanation** from Adam and Eve, and Cain, **The LORD** made us understand the need for **Accounting**, the 2nd oldest profession.

Remember that the subject or center of gravity for **Management** and **Accounting** is **Economics**. In **Economics**, our major concern is the use of our resources (gifts of **Time, Talent, and Treasure**) mindful that we have a need to compare the **benefits we may gain** with what **cost and losses we may suffer.**

<u>For what does it profit a man to gain the whole world and forfeit his soul? – Mark 8:36</u>

As in the case of the Master who entrusted his workers with TALENTS, the absentee owners who had entrusted **Management** with **Economic** resources would demand **Accounting** for such resources.

ASSETS & ALL OTHER ACCOUNTS: GAAP CODES & DEFINITIONS

Businesses had come to call such resources, **Assets**, <u>**if they satisfy**</u> the following requirements:

1) <u>They are **property**</u>, meaning that *rights* can be recognized by the state as belonging to *any legal owner*,

2) <u>They are **of value**</u> or have **_value_** or *measurable worth* in the applicable currency, and

3) <u>They can be established as **owned by the Entity**</u>.

Definitions of codes or accounts such as this one, are an integral part of the **GAAP**. Thus, **Accounting** professionals are enabled to properly **do the IMP** for the **Economic** elements that are subject to **disclosure** in **Accounting** Reports.

To explain, in the case of an ocean, source of resources for FISHERS, only fish caught are **Assets**. The ocean which is a government territory, not subject to legal ownership of individuals or business organizations cannot be included as **Assets** of any business organization.

If parts of the shores are used by the **Entity** and the **Entity** is by the governmental unit allowed exclusive use or occupancy by way of paid concessions or grants, the cost of the concession and other costs relating to occupancy, not the shores, are **Assets**.

Similarly, National Forests are not **Assets** of a lumber business even when a government agency opens them for some kind of concessions. **Assets** may be recorded only for paid concessions or lumber already legally harvested.

Illegally acquired items are not **Assets** despite possession due to lack of compliance with the "property" requirement for **Assets**.

In regard to the 2nd requirement the desired or planned benefits from extracted resources that are not reasonably measurable are not **Assets**.

In regard to the 3rd requirement, if the **Entity** cannot establish legal ownership, the items cannot be included as **Assets** by the **Entity.**

There may be **Claims** against **Assets,** whether particular or general. For example, the business organization bought an expensive equipment, making a down payment and additional payments, ownership may not transfer readily to the buyer. The seller may retain ownership or lien or the title (a particular claim of the seller) until fully paid and title transfer is documented.

Or, in the absence of a lien, especially if there are many items purchased from a certain supplier, the Entity just had a liability to the seller (a general claim of the seller) of the not fully paid items. If such Claims exist, then these Claims in effect, reduce the value of the Assets recorded.

Claims may be of outsiders called **Liabilities** or of insiders called **OWNER'S EQUITY.**

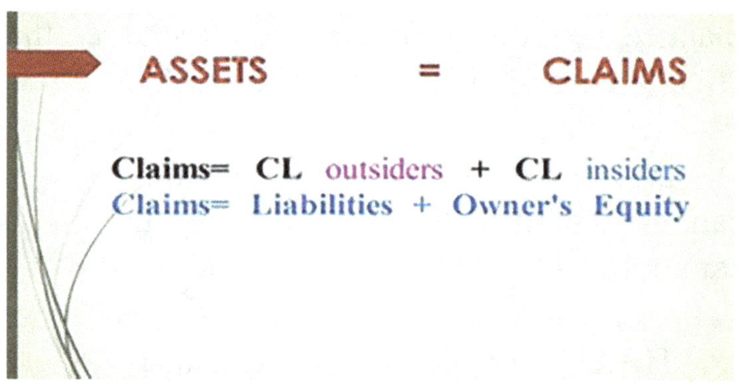

A **LIABILITY** is a legal claim of outsiders against the Entity. To be recognized or recorded, such legal claim should exist and should be capable of being **established as existent** (confirmed by the claimant and properly documented) and capable of being **measured**.

The difference between **Assets** and **Liabilities** is called Net Worth or Owner's /s' Equity.

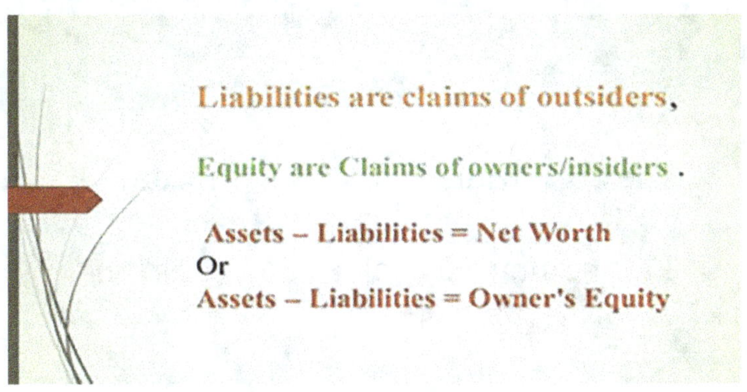

The Report showing
Assets = **Liabilities** + **Owners' Equity**
is called a **Balance Sheet** (good for a day).

This is a picture that is good for an instant (except that the legal minimum measure of time is a day).

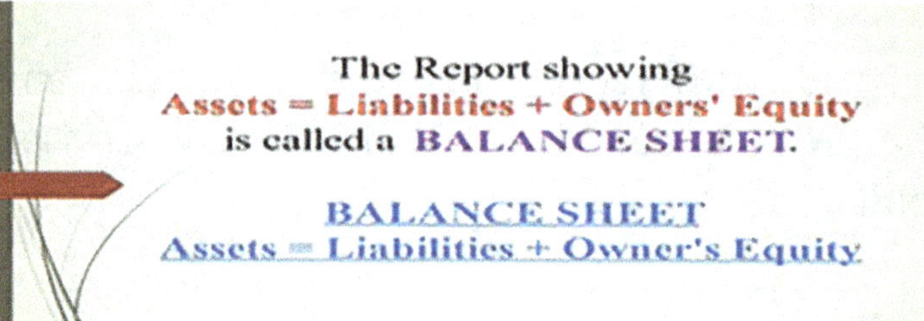

The organizations or Entities record:

1) the monetary value of services rendered as **REVENUE**

2) the monetary value of sacrifices (in form of Assets given and Liabilities assumed) for goods and services received as **COST**

3) the monetary value of expired costs as **EXPENSES**, and the monetary value of unexpired costs as Assets.

The Report showing the performance of the Entity is called **INCOME STATEMENT** (good for a period) – except that the standard business period is a year.

ACCOUNTING THE 2ND OLDEST PROFESSION

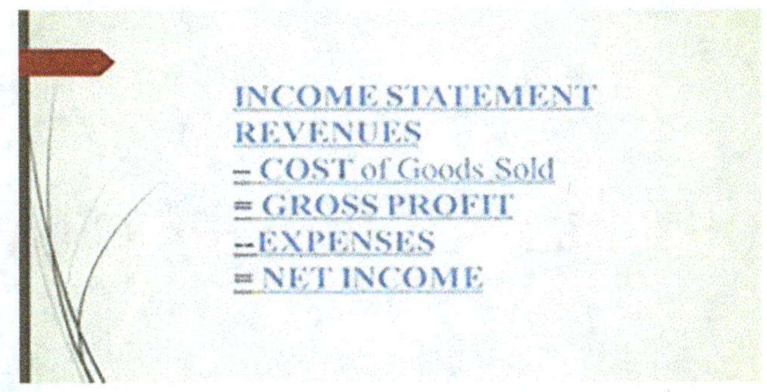

COST PRINCIPLE: 5TH GAAP

Assets may be acquired by 1) purchase (buying) or 2) manufacturing (converting) goods to other forms before selling. This pervasive **COST PRINCIPLE** requires that the **Assets** acquired be recorded at **Cost** at acquisition or conversion *(the market value of the sacrifice 1) to obtain the item and 2) to prepare it for its intended use)*.

It does not matter what form, whether it is tangible (cash or goods) or 2) intangible (service or promises as in a **Liability**) was the **SACRIFICE** to acquire the new items that had become **Assets**. Timing is important-- whether it is by purchase or conversion that the new items had become **Assets**.

REVENUE REALIZATION PRINCIPLE: 6TH GAAP

Revenues measure in monetary terms the value of services rendered. Only services rendered through: 1) delivery of goods or delivery of services, do we measure the **accomplishments of, or benefits to**, the Entity in various forms: 1) monies received, 2) goods received, 3) monies or goods to be received, and also 4) **Liabilities** forgiven.

The **REVENUE REALIZATION PRINCIPLE** requires that **Revenues** or **Income** be recognized and recorded only when earned. This principle gives guidance on the proper **measurement** and **timing** of **Revenues** of various types for various types of business or industry.

MATCHING PRINCIPLE: 7TH GAAP

EXPENSES are expired **Costs** and **Cost of Goods Sold**. **Costs** of all acquired items are initially recorded as **Assets**, as measured at acquisition, by purchase or conversion or manufacture.

Then, the **Costs** of **Assets** whose values had expired are called **EXPENSES**. What values are left unexpired remains as **Assets** for the **Entity**.

The **MATCHING PRINCIPLE** requires that at the end of the **Accounting** period, (a year or any part of the year), **EXPENSES** are to be deducted from **REVENUES** only of the **same nature** and the **same period**. This will allow the **Entity** to report its **NET INCOME** for the **Accounting** period.

The **NET INCOME** is the accepted measure of the **Entity**'s accomplishment.

CONSERVATISM PRINCIPLE: 8TH GAAP

Accountants do a lot of measurements, mostly estimates in **Accounting**. It is not uncommon that even reasonable professionals would have disagreements and differences in estimates, significant or not.

Let's take a look at this:

THE PARABLE OF THE PHARISEE AND THE TAX COLLECTOR

He (**The LORD**) then addressed this parable to those who were convinced of their own righteousness and despised everyone else.

"Two people went up to the temple area to pray; one was a Pharisee and the other was a sinner, a tax collector.

The Pharisee took up his position and spoke this prayer to himself, 'O God, I thank you that I am not like the rest of humanity -greedy, dishonest, adulterous- or even like this tax collector…I fast twice a week, and I pay tithes on my whole **Income**.'

But the tax collector stood off at a distance and would not even raise his eyes to heaven but beat his breast and prayed, 'O God, be merciful to me a sinner.'

I tell you, the latter went home justified, not the former; for everyone who exalts himself will be humbled, and the one who humbles himself will be exalted."

Here, we were observing two persons who have ideas on how they value themselves in the eyes of **The LORD** …The self-righteous man has so overvalued himself, and the tax collector, generally considered a sinner, has undervalued himself.

In **Accounting**, as we attach or assign estimated values to our **Assets** (and immediate or current period **Income**), **GAAP** prefer to err in the direction of undervaluing (or understating, underreporting) rather than overvaluing (or overstating, overreporting) our **Assets** and immediate **Income** (this year's **Income**).

Students, get to learn about the pervasive (**GAAP**) of **CONSERVATISM**. We do not intentionally engage in undervaluation and misstatements or reporting erroneous data, for we do not encourage falsehoods and lies. We press for supporting documents, calculations, evidence, and proofs for veracity and truth in our recording and reporting. But with regard to estimates, we adhere to the **GAAP**, i.e., **CONSERVATISM PRINCIPLE.**

INDUSTRY PECULIARITY PRINCIPLE: 9TH GAAP

A special Accounting Principle, it says that each industry has a special set of GAAP.

We have seen here 9 PERVASIVE ACCOUNTING PRINCIPLES, 8 of which has Scriptural basis, the last one being a late comer. They are called PERVASIVE PRINCIPLES because they are applicable to all accounts and Entities and they pervade most Accounting issues.

To summarize, here is a Chart that shows the 9 PERVASIVE GAAP.

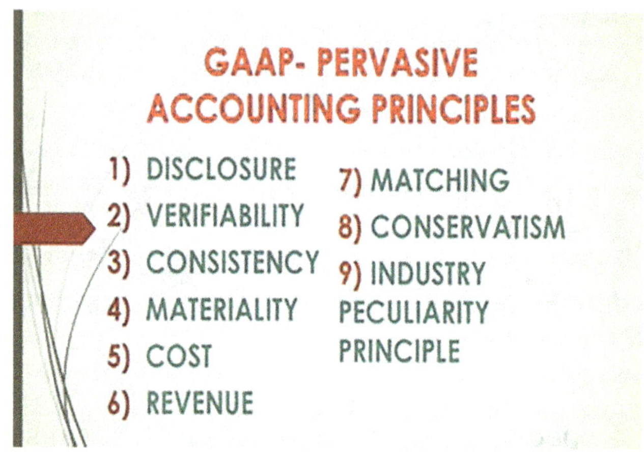

On the next page is a Chart with a quick and simple **explanation** of the **9 PERVASIVE GAAP.**

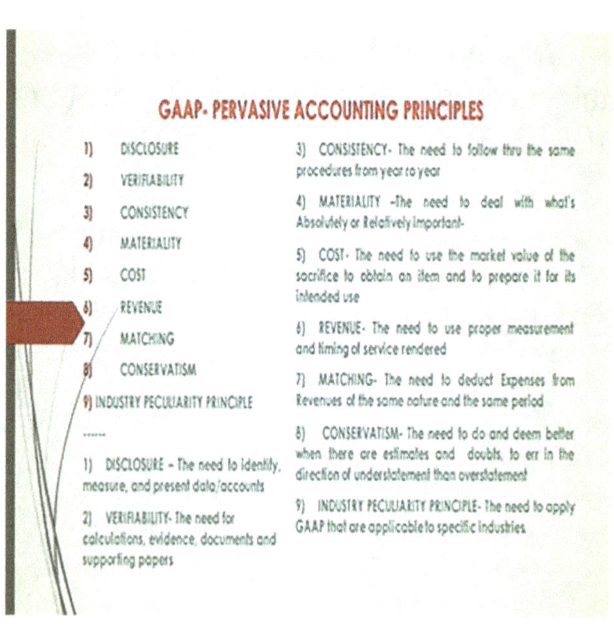

OTHER LOWER-LEVEL GAAP

Besides the PERVASIVE PRINCIPLES, there are lower-level GAAP that are called **BROAD OPERATING PRINCIPLES (BOP).** They relate to Procedures that apply to select types of **entities** and select types of Assets. For example, Accountants may be talking about alternatives like **Perpetual vs. Periodic Inventory System.**

Then there are even lower-level GAAP that are called DETAILED PRINCIPLES (DP), under a **(BOP).** They relate to Procedures that apply to some specific types of **entities** and specific types of Accounts. For example, Accountants may be talking about alternatives like **First-in, First-out (Fifo)** method vs. Last-in, First-out (Lifo) vs. **Weighted Average** method for Inventories, whether under **BOP Perpetual or Periodic Inventory System.**

In other words, the Entity may have generally adopted the **Periodic Inventory** system (**BOP**). Now, the Entity needs to elect a specific method to use among the possible (DP) may be (Fifo), so the Entity is in fact using Periodic Fifo method.

These and other lower-level GAAP are going to be covered in another volume.

In FINANCIAL Accounting, GAAP are required, as Management needs to report to outsiders and absentee owners. While Management pays the CPAs' fees, the CPAs are independent of Management. Thus. Management has no influence over the preparation of the reports. While many assume that "Whoever pays the piper calls the tune," not so with FINANCIAL Accounting reports, which need to be in accord with GAAP, which come with three levels:

1) Pervasive Principles (PP);
2) Broad Operating Principles (BOP), and
3) Detailed Principles (DP).

MANAGERIAL ACCOUNTING

2) **MANAGERIAL** Accounting reports are for internal users – data used by Managers and decision-makers. Reports are not certified by CPAs, since they are reports by, to, and for Management. Such reports are in accord with the needs and desires of Management (where, whoever pays the piper may call the tune) unlike FINANCIAL Accounting reports which need to be in accord with GAAP (where, whoever pays the piper may not necessarily call the tune).

As FINANCIAL Accounting reports are historical, or for past periods, MANAGERIAL Accounting reports may be

1) historic,
2) current, or
3) futuristic reports (projections, forecasts, budgets for future periods, whether short or long- term.)

MANAGERIAL Accounting reports, needless to say will involve details that relate to Management functions-(PODC)

1) from **P**lanning (budgets, forecasts)
2) to **O**rganizing and operating (current transactions, cost Accounting)
3) to **D**irecting and decision-making (various alternatives)
4) to **C**ontrolling and evaluating (reviews, evaluations, revisions).

COMPLIANCE ACCOUNTING

3) COMPLIANCE Accounting are reports of Managers to regulators that require them, whether with legal or trust or contractual authority. Managers need to comply by submitting Reports in special forms (like forms for the IRS) and during the time period specified (like the April 15 deadline). They are usually, albeit not always, certified by CPAs. There may be several regulatory agencies that require Reports with more details than regular FINANCIAL Accounting Reports.

These reports are for external users: different regulators with different requirements, whether legal or contractual. And there will always be people or clients complaining about the regulatory agencies.

PAYING TAXES TO THE EMPEROR

Then the Pharisees went off and plotted how they might entrap him in speech…They sent their disciples to him, with the Herodians, saying, "Teacher, we know that you are a truthful man and that you teach the way of God in accordance with the truth. And you are not concerned with anyone's opinion, for you do not regard a person's status. Tell us, then, what is your opinion: Is it lawful to pay the census tax to Caesar or not?"

Knowing their malice, Jesus said, "Why are you testing me, you hypocrites? Show me the coin that pays the census tax."…Then they handed him the Roman coin. He said to them, "Whose image is this and whose inscription?" …They replied, "Caesar's." …At than he said to them, "Then repay to Caesar what belongs to Caesar and to God what belongs to God." …When they heard this, they were amazed, and leaving him they went away.

With this lesson from **The LORD**, not even **Accounting** should help those who want to evade taxes. **The LORD** is clear on the importance of **COMPLIANCE ACCOUNTING.**

CONFIDENTIALITY

Most **Accounting** information are confidential. Such should not be provided to anyone not legally entitled to such information. There will always be tricksters that would take advantage of unsuspecting providers of important information to release such to them, at the provider's peril.

We saw how the snake started to bait the woman, using a lie…Now the snake was the most cunning of all the wild animals that **The LORD God** had made. He asked the woman, "Did God really say, 'You shall not eat from any of the trees in the garden'?"

That was a trick question: the question was expressed with a lie-- "Did God really say, 'You shall not eat from any of the trees in the garden'?"

Now, we should have learned from the experience in the Garden not to provide information to those who may not be entitled lest we find ourselves aiding spies or enemies or saboteurs, just trying to fish for information that they could use to harm us in any way.

With **Management** as the 1ˢᵗ and oldest profession and **Accounting** as the 2ⁿᵈ oldest profession, to which we are called, it is for us to decide if we want to heed the call.

Anyone planning to become head of a family better be prepared to do **Management.** Middle School education historically had courses in Home Economics. Young students could use guidance from teachers, parents, elders of the community, from those who are issuing marriage licenses and those officiating marriage ceremonies.

We were given by **The LORD** such dominion or authority, albeit limited, to manage resources, given to us, of varying types and amounts, namely, **TIME, TALENT,** and **TREASURE.** Like the servants who were given 5, 2, and 1 **TALENTS,** respectively, based on their capabilities, **The LORD** expects us to **account for the results** in relation to the provided resources. Also, we need to be mindful that to whom much is given, much is expected.

THE PARABLE OF THE WEDDING FEAST

Jesus again in reply spoke to them in parables, saying, "The kingdom of heaven may be likened to a king who gave a wedding feast for his son. He dispatched his servants to summon the invited guests to the feast, but they refused to come.

A 2nd time he sent other servants, saying, 'Tell those invited: "Behold, I have prepared my banquet, my calves and fattened cattle are killed, and everything is ready; come to the feast."'

Some ignored the invitation and went away, one to his farm, another to his business. The rest laid hold of his servants, mistreated them, and killed them…The king was enraged and sent his troops, destroyed those murderers, and burnt their city…Then he said to his servants, 'The feast is ready, but those who were invited were not worthy to come. Go out, therefore, into the main roads and invite to the feast whomever you find.'

The servants went out into the streets and gathered all they found, bad and good alike, and the hall was filled with guests…But when the king came in to meet the guests, he saw a man there not dressed in a wedding garment. He said to him, 'My friend, how is it that you came in here without a wedding garment?' But he was reduced to silence.

Then the king said to his attendants, 'Bind his hands and feet, and cast him into the darkness outside, where there will be wailing and grinding of teeth.' …Many are invited, but few are chosen."

Whatever we are called to, the least we could do is come prepared for the tasks or roles we need to play…Sooner or later, we will realize that we are called to learn Management and Accounting regardless of our primary professions and inclinations.

The Lord talks about

WORKERS IN THE VINEYARD (LIFO)

"After agreeing with them for the usual daily wage, he sent them at varying times into his vineyard... So, they went off... When it was evening the owner of the vineyard said to his foreman, 'Summon the laborers and give them their pay, beginning with the last and ending with the 1st ... each of them also got the usual wage.

And on receiving it they grumbled against the landowner, saying, 'These last ones worked only one hour, and you have made them equal to us, who bore the day's burden and the heat.' He said to one of them in reply, 'My friend, I am not cheating you. Did you not agree with me for the usual daily wage? Take what is yours and go. What if I wish to give this last one the same as you? [Or] am I not free to do as I wish with my own money? Are you envious because I am generous?'

Thus, the last will be first, and the first will be last."

Whatever is our primary profession, at whatever part of life we realize, we will face the **economic** reality that our goal is to have **BENEFITS** that exceed **COSTS.** Also, we could and should not be oblivious of our **non-economic** goals.

Let's look at this passage.

THE CONDITIONS OF DISCIPLESHIP

Ultimate Measure of Profitability: Cost Benefit Relationship

He summoned the crowd with his disciples and said to them, "Whoever wishes to come after me must deny himself, take up his cross, and follow me…For whoever wishes to save his life will lose it, but whoever loses his life for my sake and that of the gospel will save it…What profit is there for one to gain the whole world and forfeit his life? …What could one give in exchange for his life?

What does our **Economic** picture show? How do our expected **BENEFITS** compare with our expected **COSTS/ EXPENSES**? How close are we to achieving our goal?

Remember, each of us sets our goal and can set what **COST** we are willing to sacrifice or invest to reach our goal or to gain our expected BENEFITS.

Are we dressed with 1) commitment to values and principles, 2) skills to do our tasks as Managers and to do **explanation** as Accountants, 3) a big heart in the right place (not as shown by St. Anthony, for one whose heart left his body to dwell in his own treasure chest), 4) common sense and 5) good judgment. So, are we properly dressed to **come as we are called**—that **we may be chosen?**

I am a retired Accounting professional: as an Accountant (I do or did) and as an Educator (I teach or I taught). Oh yes, sorely, it has been observed that those who can't, teach.

The LORD said it too that of some, you need to do or follow **what they preach/teach rather than what they do.** This is true in and of any field.

You have just been with me thru ACCT 101. Please find my other volumes in Management and **Accounting**, including models that I had developed to provide my students with an integrated view of **Accounting Concepts and Principles.**

It is my hope that you visit virtually thru my booklets or volumes in various topics or visit actually to Aurora's Decagon at Villa Cecilia.

Sincerely,
Aurora

www.ingramcontent.com/pod-product-compliance
Lightning Source LLC
Chambersburg PA
CBHW070032260726

48658CB00002B/601